The Simple Press Company

Thank you for buying this book,
we hope you and your child gets as much
enjoyment from it as we had creating it.

If you would like updates on future books
from The Simple Press Company
or have any suggestions or ideas for books
you'd like to see please drop us an email at:

simplepresscompany@gmail.com

Also, if you did enjoy this book,
please think about leaving us a review where
you purchased the book, positive reviews really
do help independent publishers like us!

This Book Belongs To:

____

the
MAGIC
is in
YOU

YOU CAN
CHANGE
THE WORLD,
GIRL

BE
JOY
FUL

Do Not
GIVE
UP

REGRET
Nothing

HAVE
COURAGE
AND
be KIND

Stay
Humble

Think
HAPPY
thoughts

Never Stop dreaming

MISTAKES
ARE
Proof
THAT YOU ARE
TRYING

ACTUALLY
I Can

MAKE
TODAY
Amazing

Be The

Best

Version

of you

you
DESERVE
TO BE
Happy

FOLLOW YOUR OWN STAR

BE
Strong
AND
Courageous

BE
Brave
WITH YOUR
Life

do what
Brings
you
Joy

I'M NOT WEIRD I'M LIMITED EDITION

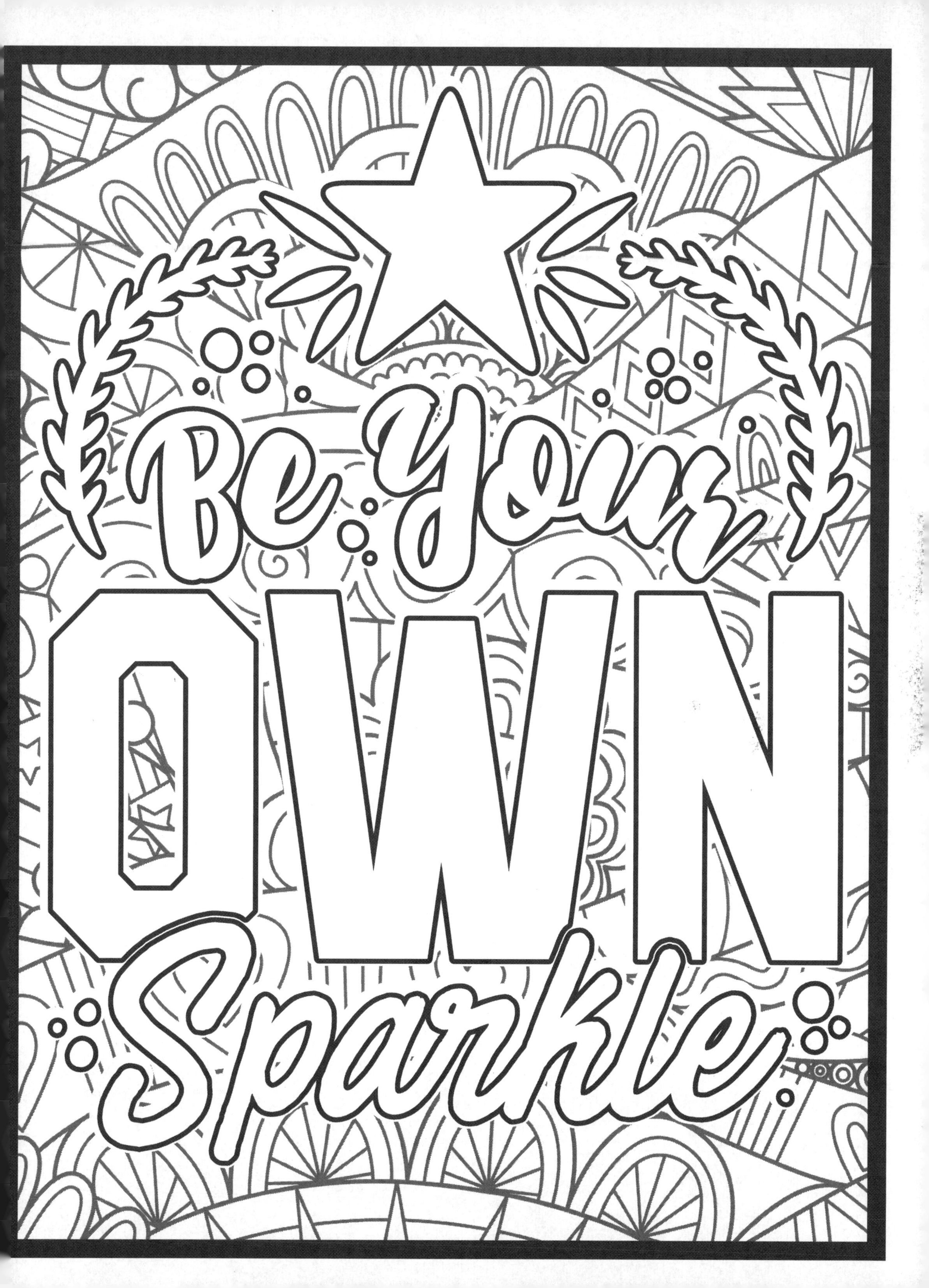
Be your
OWN
Sparkle

ALWAYS
Believe
IN
YOURSELF

Color
Me
HAPPY

Be

PROUD

OF WHO

YOU ARE

be
fearless

Yes
YOU CAN!

do what
Brings
you
Joy

I'm Very
PROUD
OF
me

GRL
PWR

I have THE Fire

FORGET
THE
Mistake
Remember
THE
LESSON

ENERGY
SPEAKS
LOUDER
THAN
WORDS

YOU ARE STRONG AS HELL

Be
PROUD
of
who you are

BE THE RAINBOW IN Someone else's CLOUD

WHEREVER
YOU ARE
BE all THERE

Think
LIKE A
PROTON
AND
STAY
POSITIVE

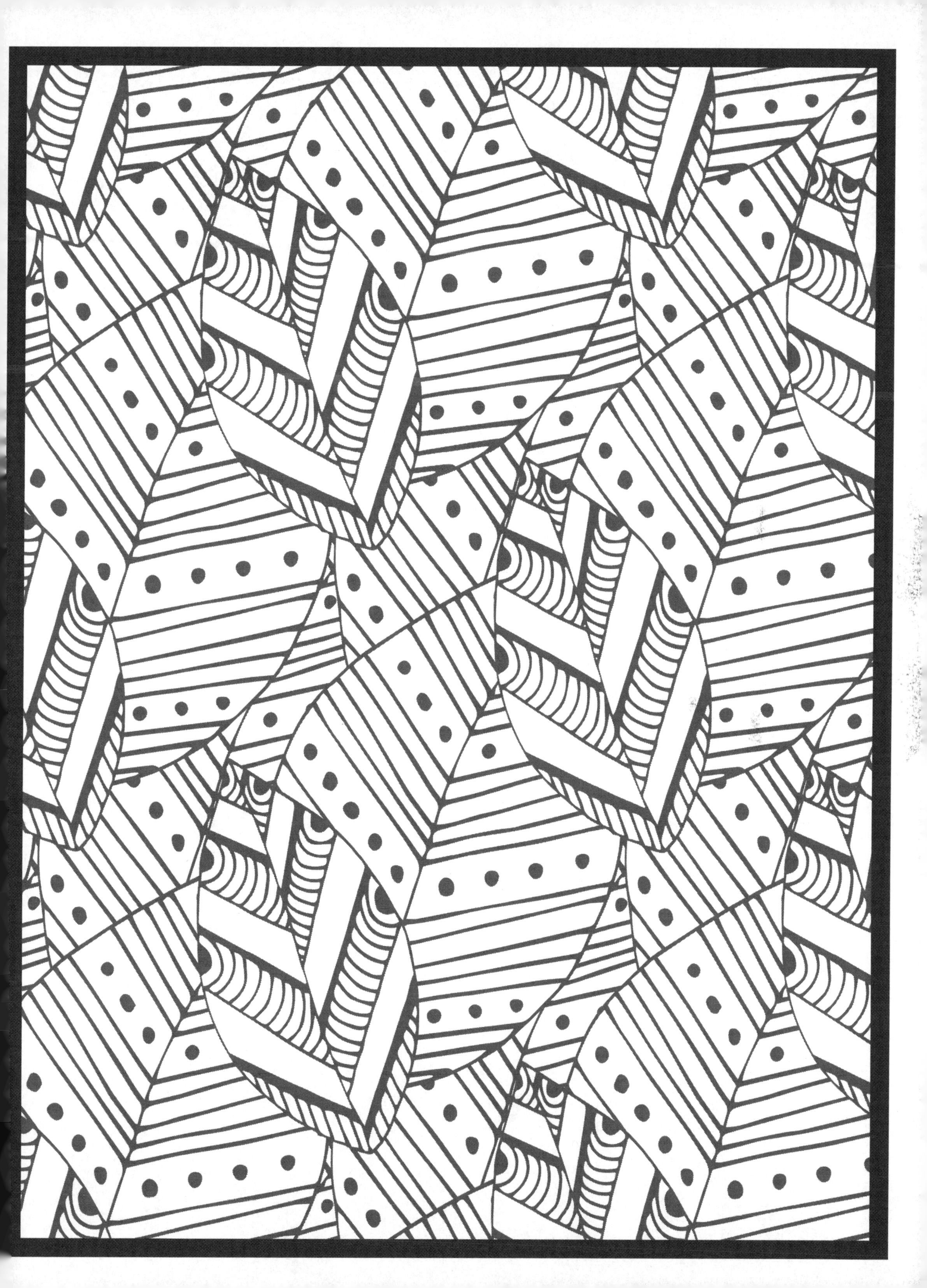

GOOD
vibes
ONLY

Only
POSITIVE
Vibes

NEVER
give up

LET'S

Explore

this

AWESOME

WORLd

Enjoy
Every
moment

let's
DO
this

YOU
ARE
WORTHY

EVERYTHING
WILL BE
OK

WHEN YOU
CAN'T FIND THE
SUNSHINE
BE THE SUNSHINE

THE WORLD
Needs
MORE
more
YOU

IT'S HARD

to

Beat

A PERSON

who never

Give up

I can
and
I will

Made in the USA
Las Vegas, NV
20 November 2024

12169061R00057